LOOK CLOSE
SEE FAR

LOOK CLOSE
SEE FAR

A CULTURAL PORTRAIT OF THE MAYA

PHOTOGRAPHS BY BRUCE T. MARTIN

GEORGE BRAZILLER / NEW YORK

Published in 2007 by George Braziller, Inc.

For information, please address the publisher:
George Braziller, Inc.
171 Madison Avenue
New York, NY 10016

Library of Congress Cataloging-in-Publication Data
Martin, Bruce T., 1955–
Look close, see far : images of the Maya / photographs by Bruce T.
Martin.—1st ed.
          p. cm.
Includes bibliographical references.
ISBN 978-0-8076-1589-8
1. Mayas—Social life and customs—Pictorial works. 2. Mayas—
Social conditions—Pictorial works. 3. Mayas—Antiquities—
Pictorial works. 4. Central America—Social life and customs—
Pictorial works. 5. Central America—Social conditions—Pictorial
works. 6. Central America—Antiquities—Pictorial works. I. Title.
F1435.3.S7M367 2007
972.81—dc22
                    2007012920

Designed by Rita Lascaro
Frontispiece: Tulum, Quintana Roo, Mexico, 1987
Printed and bound in Singapore

First edition

CONTENTS

ACKNOWLEDGMENTS

I am grateful to many people for their support during this twenty-year journey in Central America. My wife and children, Ina, Hannah, and Zachary, have been a constant source of inspiration. Dave Munroe, president of the Compass Club, has been a valuable traveling partner. Without the help of studio managers Meghan Scott and Mollie Laurienzo, this book would not have been possible.

My thanks to Allen Christenson, Patricia McAnany, Shoshaunna Parks, David Freidel, and Marianna Kunow for their writing and insights into the Maya. My appreciation also to other Maya experts who helped along the way: Elin Danien, Linda Schele, William Fash, Robert Shearer, Rosemary Joyce, Leticia Roche, and Oscar Cruz Melgar, along with the Belize National Institute of Culture and History, the Guatemalan Instituto de Antropología e Historia, the Honduran Instituto de Antropología, and the Mexican Instituto National de Antropología e Historia.

I have benefited from the help of Mark Beckstrand, Glenn Engman, Dave Kurtis, Sara Churchill, Alex Winsby, Tim Harper, Dana Salvo, Jim Ringel, Jerry Rabinowitz, Ellen Rothenberg, Dan Orlow, Steve Fowler, Edmund Griffen, Keith Brodie, John Moore, Rob Martin, Pam Wilson, Mike Conway, Joe Federico, Ned Flood, Dave Herrick, Dan Smagreolio, Brian Walsh, and the many Maya people I met along the way who showed me much and taught me more.

I thank George Braziller for his support in choosing this project to publish, and for its completion, my thanks to Jessica Benko.

I would like to dedicate this book to my parents,
Mildred and Ansel Martin,
for all of their help and support over the years,
and to the Maya people in their struggle
to maintain their cultural dignity.

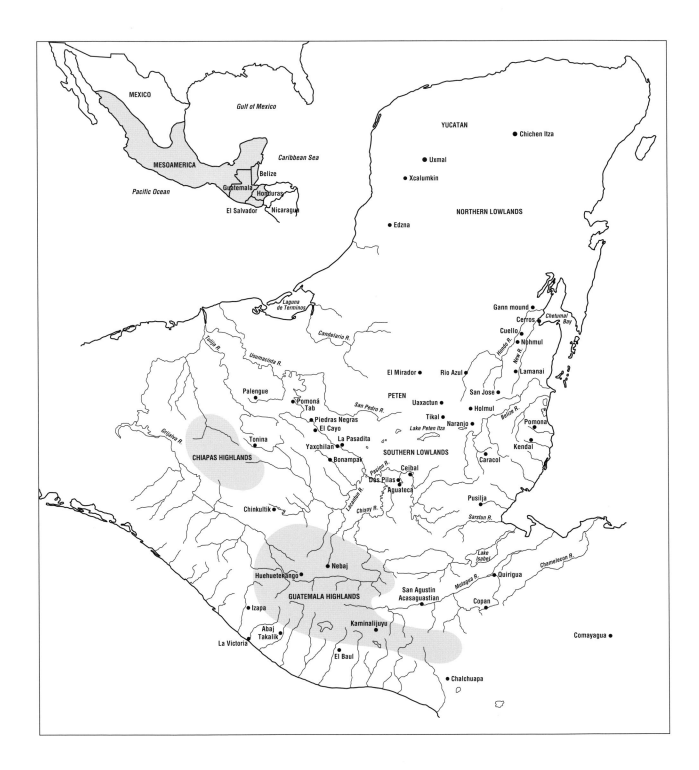

MEXICO

Gulf of Mexico

MESOAMERICA

Caribbean Sea

Pacific Ocean

Belize

Guatemala

Honduras

El Salvador

Nicaragua

YUCATAN

● Chichen Itza

● Uxmal

● Xcalumkin

NORTHERN LOWLANDS

● Edzna

Laguna
de Terminos

Candelario R.

Gann mound ●

Cerros ●

Chetumal
Bay

Cuello ●

Hondo R.

● Nohmul

New R.

Tzilja R.

Usumacinta R.

● El Mirador   ● Rio Azul

● Lamanai

Palengue ●

● Pomoná
   Tab

San Pedro R.

PETEN

Uaxactun ●

● San Jose

● Piedras Negras

● El Cayo

Tikal ●

● Holmul

Belize R.

● Pomona

Grijalva R.

Tonina ●

● La Pasadita

● Yaxchilan

Naranjo ●

● Kendal

CHIAPAS HIGHLANDS

● Bonampak

SOUTHERN LOWLANDS

● Caracol

Pasion R.

Ceibal ●

Dos Pilas ●

● Aguateca

● Pusilja

Chinkultik ●

Lacanlun R.

Chixoy R.

Sarstun R.

Lake
Isabel

Chamelecon R.

● Nebaj

Huehuetenango ●

GUATEMALA HIGHLANDS

San Agustin
Acasaguastian ●

Motagua R.

● Quirigua

● Izapa

Kaminalijuyu ●

● Copan

Abaj
Takalik ●

● Comayagua

La Victoria ●

● El Baul

● Chalchuapa

FOREWORD

When I first looked at Bruce Martin's photographs, I understood that he was someone who had spent a very long time finding the moments, the people, and the places of these portraits, capturing their elusive, transcendent, and immediate qualities and imprinting them with the care and craft required of photography when it is art and not just chronicle. These images convey a personal connection and experience. I recognize the Maya people I know through these photographs. I see friends who have walked forest paths with me, sometimes chuckling at a joke, sometimes pointing out a healing plant, sometimes just talking about how things are. I see *halach winikob*, real people, elders who have sat in the shade with me and guided me to an understanding of village politics, of the complex array of churches and faiths, and of their hopes for their children's futures. I see the farmers who strain their eyes to find the clouds on the horizon, willing them to pass over their fields in the dusty heat of afternoon with fresh, cool sweeping rain.

If there is anything that is fundamentally enduring across centuries of change in the land of the Maya, it is the perception that the world and all of the creatures and objects it contains are alive, pervasively sentient, and endowed with divine spirit. Maya people I know do not mistake the images of saints, crosses, and transcendent modern deities like San Simon, or Maximón, for the beings they represent. But they do believe that like their own bodies, such images can and do house mindful spirits. I recall watching a shaman-priest in the church of Chichicastenango prepare offerings of flowers and candles for his ill client, and then carefully knock on the base of the altar before addressing the saint whose image stood above, politely making sure the saint

---

OPPOSITE: *Mayan region of Central America*

9

was home before addressing him with prayer. The town saints are surely present when their images, resplendently adorned, process through the market during Holy Week accompanied by ear-splitting blasts of celebratory black powder fireworks. San Simon holds court for his supplicants, enjoying his cigars and cigarettes, his liquor and his prayers. Fortunes, happiness, love, and darker desires all are cradled in his outstretched palm. Hope is a booming industry in his shrines, frequented by adepts hawking burnt offerings and miracles. His annual encounter with Christ during Holy Week in Santiago Atitlán, the dance of their images amid the throngs of people, is high drama of the most poignant kind and inspiration for me when I am imagining past pageants on the quiet, empty plazas of ancient cities in the Petén. Among the people of Yucatán, the green painted crosses, with their dresses and sashes, are just as alive, and sometimes they speak to their congregants. The image and being of the cross-shaped World Tree was nearly two thousand years old among the Maya when the Spanish arrived with a facsimile. The crosses, and the world around them, converted to Christianity. But they never forgot their roots, deeply anchored in the mountain pyramids and fecund caves.

Loltun cave was a pilgrimage place of Maya kings at the beginning of time, and one had his image carved at the mouth of it. Like the images of contemporary saints and crosses, the images of ancient kings are wedded to their spiritual beings, and the Loltun king stands sentinel to the Underworld home of gods and ancestors. In the image on page 52, shafts of light through the main chamber fall down upon stalagmites carved into miniature pyramids with stairways up their sides, the microcosmic world of the dead. Water flows through caves like blood through the mother crocodilian Earth that carries the night sun to be reborn daily in the East. So, at least, some ancient Maya evidently believed and depicted in their art. Theirs was a world thoroughly shaped, like a living work of art, into their understanding of the creation. Maya scriptures, ancient and modern, lay on human beings the responsibility of sustaining living abodes and images of the divine. Architectural fragments of earthly art stand in Yucatán. Smooth walls and awesome god masks frame dark doorways into these elegant buildings of hard cement and limestone veneer, impressing the conquering friars even as they sought to destroy reverence for them by quarrying some for churches. In the Petén, the Classic Maya somehow failed in the task of nurturing the world, and much of the rolling hill country reverted to forest when they died or left. The images in this book capture the romance and beauty of abandonment, great tree roots coiled around blocks of stone. The huge pyramids of king Yik'in Chan K'awiil of Tikal thrust their roofs skyward above the forest canopy, still declaring victory in war, war unending and dooming to civil society.

Many of the modern Maya farm the land as their ancestors did before them, and working the fields slowly shapes the bodies of young men into maturity, before they become gnarled or flaccid as the choices of life dictate. But while they have their handsome flesh, their boundless energy explodes in twilight ballgames in the village square. Their fathers and grandfathers watch and remember being as vital as young corn. Maize, as Allen Christenson observes, is the holy sustenance, the gift of the saintly rain. To hold its kernels, to make it into thick cakes, are deeply satisfying acts of ordinary piety. Hospitality is a common virtue among the Maya I know, and some of these portraits convey welcome and tolerance. But poverty and injustice are brutal masters, and they etch anger and anguish on Maya faces as they do on those of other victims. Some of these portraits of Maya women show the worry and the indomitable determination to cope and survive that are birthed along with children into an uncertain world. I have seen in Yaxuna village, Yucatán, Don Emetario's granddaughter Daisy grow from a childhood friend of my daughters to a wife and mother, from a bright young girl with plans to engage the outside world, to a pillar of the most traditional hamlet in her village.

The real choices about identity are painful and take courage to live with. Oppression is now centuries old, as pervasive and transparent as air and the words conveyed through it. I once struck up a conversation in my fledgling Yucatec with a woman working in Piste, the town next to Chichen Itza, and said I thought the language was beautiful. She disagreed, and said that the real Mayan was spoken far away, in Guatemala. Yet for all the hardship, the cycle of Maya life is the true immortality. In another of this book's compelling tableaus (page 114), the old Chortí grandfather's eyes may have withered, no longer able to see the Copán kings, the European conquerors, or the tourists, but his granddaughter's gaze is true and consoling. Bruce Martin's photographs allow us to witness the remnants of the Maya culture's past, the reality of its present, and the hope for its future. Seeing through his lens lets us believe in it.

—David Freidel, Ph.D.

11

INTRODUCTION

Look Close See Far: *A Cultural Portrait of the Maya* examines the Maya region of Central America, an area both beautiful and complex. It is a place where a fragile balance between society and the natural world dominates life and the endurance of the unique Maya worldview challenges one's understanding of reality. Since 1987, I have taken more than ten thousand photographs over a range of landscapes and communities in an attempt to make a distinctive portrait of this singular culture.

These images are of the Maya Indians of Belize, Guatemala, Honduras, and southern Mexico. In their communities in Central America today, some Maya still revere their pre-Columbian earth lords, ritually consult their deceased ancestors, and struggle daily to respect their cultural heritage while adapting to the pace and changes of contemporary lifestyles. Rapid development in recent years has introduced contrasting and sometimes violent influences, which threaten to overwhelm the Maya and their environment. Surviving these disruptive influences and protecting their cultural dignity are the challenges for an uncertain future the Maya now face.

Searching through the incredible landscapes, ruins, and cultures of this diverse network of communities, I have photographed elements that represent Maya groups and their traditional worldview. These elements include artifacts from the past, details of daily life, and conceptual images that reveal the Maya experience. These visual components can be found in the Maya's iconographic remains in the jungle landscapes at such sites as Aguateca, Altun Ha, Arroyo de Piedras, Coba, Copán, Dos Pilas, Edzná, Labná, Palanque, Piedras Negras, Sayil, Ceibal, Tikal, Tulum, Uxmal, Yaxchilán, and Yaxhá, as well as among the contemporary highland villagers of Guatemala; the Santa Cruz Maya of southern Belize; the subsistence farmers of Maní, Mexico; and the members of rural communities in the Petén of Guatemala. The photographs concentrate on symbols representing the eternal cycles of Maya life and religion, their relationship to the land, and the influences imposed on them by sixteenth-century Spanish conquistadors and modern cultures between then and now.

Among the narrow trails winding among restored structures at many Maya ruins, there are many uncovered mounds that remain to be excavated. These ruins throughout the Maya region keep the history of the past inhabitants in their stone carvings, buried tombs, and crumbled architecture. The green, often wet, canopy that covers the sites provides a lush background for witnessing carvings and structures that have been abandoned to time. The writings and the weathered depictions of ancient faces and elaborate dress found on limestone sculptures and buried ceramics throughout these hilly ceremonial centers chronicle the Maya ancestors' history and worldview through iconic imagery. These symbols, transmitted and modified from generation to generation through myths and rituals, are the cultural signposts by which members of these societies navigate their lives and justify their actions, even today.

To many contemporary Maya, time is a living dimension in which each day has a unique personality. They conceive of time as cyclical, with history continually repeating itself with different players and rhythms. The tropical forest is important to the Maya both as a physical resource and as a sacred guide for spiritual renewal. Today, the Central American rainforest is disappearing at an epidemic rate of over 700,000 acres per year, according to the Food and Agriculture Organization of the United Nations. Traditional farming methods, such as slash and burn, are still used all over the region. This is a low cost way to fertilize land, but it exacerbates soil erosion, the greenhouse effect, and deforestation. Subsistence farming provides a limited amount of food to support a family. A good harvest might produce extra food for barter, but a poor one can leave the family undernourished and destitute. Inadequate health care and education have led to high rates of illiteracy, infant mortality, and poverty all over the region. Challenges to the preservation and integration of distinctive Maya heritage abound in the face of these contemporary influences, pressures, and realities. Before the Maya's endangered way of life disappears completely, it is essential to attempt to understand the culture and heritage of these people and what they represent.

I am motivated to use photography to document our world, explore our perceptions, and question our viewpoints. *Look Close, See Far: A Cultural Portrait of the Maya* can help us to compare the unique Maya worldview to the foundational myths of our own society. The Maya people struggle to understand and maintain a connection to their heritage and the rich histories of their people while working to improve education, healthcare, and financial sustainability in their communities in a modern context. The future for them is unclear. Surviving the twenty-first century had become the greatest challenge the Maya culture has ever faced. I hope this project can contribute to a greater appreciation of Maya heritage, a heightened awareness of the issues the Maya are grappling with today, a more productive dialogue on their plight, and increased respect for fading Maya traditions.

—Bruce T. Martin

RECLAIMING MAYA ANCESTRY

by Shoshaunna Parks and Patricia A. McAnany, Ph.D.

The majesty of ancestral Maya archaeological cities—many featured in the pages of this book—is virtually unparalleled in the Americas. Yet the pyramids and palaces, many crumbling beneath the weight of hundreds of years of abandonment, suggest that their builders—Maya people—are something from the past, inaccessible or nonexistent in the present. Each year, thousands of tourists visit ruins such as those in Copán in western Honduras, but they rarely connect the architectural goliaths of ancestral Maya civilization with the weathered subsistence farmers and the women who sell *recuerdos*—tourist mementos—from sidewalk stalls. Instead, most wonder what happened to the ancient Maya. Where are the astronomers, the writers of complex hieroglyphics, the semidivine lords and ladies who sat on jaguar thrones? Why did they "disappear," leaving behind such an incredible cultural legacy? The truth, of course, is that Maya society never disappeared; rather, like complex social forms throughout the world and through time, Maya civilization has undergone many transformations, the most unfortunate of which began when Spanish galleons appeared on the horizon in the sixteenth century. We propose that European colonization of the Maya world—followed by a period of independent nation building—conspired to tear asunder the links between Maya peoples and their ancestral past. We also delve into how this occurred and how contemporary Maya people are working to reclaim the sacred sites and spiritual power of their ancestors.

Classical Maya civilization is rooted in a pre-Classic period (1200 BC–AD 250), which is marked by the emergence of political hierarchy and social "speciation" during which powerful individuals were able to command the labor

---

OPPOSITE: *Piedras Negras, Rio Usumacinta, El Petén, Guatemala, 2001*

and resources necessary for construction of architectural projects on a monumental scale. Contrary to the impression we have of the Maya today—due to the superior preservation of stone-faced palaces and temple-pyramids, as opposed to ordinary perishable houses and small earthen residential mounds—most ancestral Maya peoples were neither wealthy nor possessed specialized knowledge of hieroglyphic writing or astronomy. These highly advanced elements of pre-Classic and Classic Maya society were restricted to the überelite and the spiritual leaders of society, and were not accessible to the majority of Maya people.

The Classic period of Maya civilization thrived for over five hundred years (AD 250–800), as powerful cities with distinct dynastic traditions emerged throughout the wet, forested lowlands of Guatemala, Belize, southern Mexico, and western Honduras. Following a well-worn pattern among archaic states worldwide, competition for limited resources led to martial tension, as kingdoms banded together to form alliances and later split apart in conflict.[1] Palaces, temple-pyramids, and stelae, or inscribed pillars, all testified to the strength of the polity's rulers and commemorated the achievements of dynastic ancestors. The "collapse" of Maya civilization between the eighth and tenth centuries—the apocalyptic event often touted as the downfall of the powerful Classic Maya—was no collapse at all, but rather was a profound transformation of the political and economic ethos according to which power was distributed. Although the great dynastic cities of the Classic period were largely depopulated between the eighth and tenth centuries, and significant demographic shifts occurred as a result, Maya culture survived as it had for thousands of years.

Many people—including, at times, Maya peoples themselves—conflate the concept of the Classic-period Maya collapse with the arrival of Spanish conquistadors in the mid-sixteenth century. With over five hundred years between the two events, few, if any, significant parallels can be drawn between them. The earlier societal transformations stemmed from internal changes that took place within Mesoamerica during the eighth, ninth, and tenth centuries. Structures of governance eroded as a result of martial conflict, a growing population, and trends toward decentralization that followed in the wake of the decline of the great highland city of Teotihuacan. While the power of lowland cities such as Tikal and Altun Ha waned, other polities, including Sayil and

Chichén Itzá, emerged or were revitalized with new concentrations of wealth and power in the drier northern Yucatán peninsula and along strategic trade corridors. Maya populations in the lowlands and highlands of Belize, Guatemala, Honduras, Mexico, and El Salvador reacted to the breakdown of former political centers by distributing themselves more evenly across the landscape, but they continued to make pilgrimages to the powerful places of their ancestors, which had become spiritual and sacred sites.[2]

By contrast, the changes that took place following the arrival of Europeans in the Americas represent the imposition of an altogether foreign ethos of conquest and Christianization. Perhaps most significantly, many millions of Maya people—particularly those leaders in direct negotiations and conflict with Spaniards—were decimated by warfare and foreign pathogens, leaving behind a decidedly smaller and no doubt emotionally devastated society. Those who once constructed El Castillo at Xunantunich, Belize, and the intricately carved monuments of Dos Pilas, Guatemala, without a single metal tool or beast of burden, were now at the mercy of a small band of Europeans who dominated them with technology and brutality the likes of which they had never before encountered. The sovereignty that Maya peoples had enjoyed over two thousand years of civilization was subordinated to new forms of European governance forcibly imposed on them during the sixteenth century.

Despite the assault of colonization on Maya populations throughout Mesoamerica, myriad languages and traditions of the Maya people survived. Today, over five million people, comprising at least thirty distinct ethnolinguistic groups, reside in Mexico, Guatemala, Belize, and Honduras. Many Maya communities maintain a language, style of dress (or *traje*), and spiritual traditions that represent a synergism of pre- and post-sixteenth-century social practices. Others, notably in western Honduras, eastern Guatemala, and northern and western Belize, experienced a type of colonialism and postcolonialism that left them disenfranchised and disconnected from the practices and ethos of pre-Hispanic Maya peoples. Still others, such as the Mopan and Q'eqchi' Maya communities in southern Belize, maintain distinctive cultural traditions of language and dress, yet feel little connection to their pre-Hispanic predecessors.

Three of the individuals Bruce Martin photographed in 1998 (pp. 133–135) are part of one community of Maya peoples whose knowledge of their connection to the pre-Hispanic past has been all but severed. Seven years after Martin encountered the young Mopan Maya women and their children at the ruins of Uxbenká in southern Belize, one of us (Parks) embarked on anthropological field research in the nearby village of Santa Cruz. Friendly and talkative, these women quickly became some of the author's closest confidants in the community. Two of them were the mothers of multiple children; one had never married or borne children and, at age twenty-seven, probably never would. Their roles within the household revolved around the successful maintenance of their families, including the transmission of cultural traditions such as the Mopan Maya language, food-preparation techniques (especially the production of corn tortillas), and craft making. Yet, in their many conversations about their sense of connection to their Maya ancestors, these women revealed that, although they conduct their lives as "Maya," they were not the same as the "old" Maya, though what the differences were exactly, they did not know. Never having been formally taught about their ancestral past and living in a community where oral histories have all but disappeared, they simply could not see how men who could move huge boulders to build massive pyramids—men who did not believe in a Christian God—could be the same as the god-fearing subsistence farmers who today call themselves "Maya." While many community members recognize that the ancient Maya are like the roots of the family tree of contemporary Mopan Maya people, cultural heritage or ancestry neither defines their identity nor affects the way in which they conduct their lives spiritually or culturally. This contrasts greatly with some highland Maya groups who actively claim ancestral places as their own.

There is irony in the hesitancy among some Maya peoples to claim or even recognize their descent from those of deep, ancestral time. Many archaeologists consider reverence for the ancestors to have been a defining trait of pre-Hispanic Maya civilization. One of us (McAnany) has noted that it was not only through the construction of royal tombs that ancestors were commemorated but also through interment beneath house floors.[3] This practice of *living with the ancestors* lent a note of conservatism to Maya society but it also helped to chart a course for the future. It was through ancestors and the matrix of kinship that one's identity as well as rights, privileges, and social obligations were defined. In Maya deep history, ancestors were intimately entwined with the landscape—both the built and the natural environment. Ancestral presence loomed large, not only near the late Classic funerary pyramids but also in the residential compounds of commoners where ancestors "slept" beneath the floors of earlier constructions and in rock shelters where tombs are found. Burial sites, especially tombs, were revisited and additional offerings placed near ancestral human remains; this has been documented for a royal tomb built within a structure called Margarita, where a female weaver (and probable wife of dynastic founder, K'inich Yax K'uk' Mo') died in the fifth century at Copán, Honduras.[4]

The severing of the link between Maya peoples and their pre-Hispanic ancestors is tied to the experience of colonization and postcolonialism, most recently influenced by the process of nation building. Large and small archaeological sites, ubiquitous reminders of an ancestral Maya landscape, are identified and managed under the national laws of Mexico, Guatemala, Honduras, and Belize as the property of the state. National pride is rooted in these locales; they provide legitimate evidence of the great past of an equally great modern country.[5] In defining these sites as sources of national heritage, however, we must consider the national identity of the population of the country: Who belongs and who is excluded?

Denial of the existence of modern Maya groups has been part of official social and political discourse—both intentional and unintentional—throughout the postcolonial period. In Guatemala as late as the 1990s, official government censuses indicated that only approximately 36 percent of the population belonged to a Maya ethnic group, compared to estimates of around 50–60 percent from alternative (nongovernmental) censuses of the 1990s.[6] Unfortunately, popular accounts as well as archaeological investigations into pre-Hispanic and colonial periods can and have further contributed to the myth that Maya peoples are absent from the populations of contemporary Mexico, Guatemala, Belize, and Honduras. By focusing on periods of social and political upheaval, researchers (as well as writers and filmmakers) convey the impression that indigenous peoples were destroyed or quickly assimilated into Western cultural forms.[7] National culture, therefore, cannot include Maya peoples who no longer exist.

Increasingly, however, nation-states and the international community have come to recognize the existence of Maya peoples and their right to be distinguished within multicultural national populations that celebrate diversity and respect cultural self-determination. While ethnic and/or community boundaries remain paramount to the disparate identities of Maya groups, many Maya descendants now see themselves as part of an "imagined community"[8] of millions of indigenous Maya people. The simple recognition of the sheer number of Maya descendants present within the region has been a vital step toward the revitalization of Maya identity and the growing interest in reclaiming Maya ancestry. The pan-Maya movement, contrary to its name, is not a unified drive on behalf of Maya leaders and descendants to gain recognition for the imagined community of Maya peoples spanning four nation-states. Instead, it is a name used to describe the swell of cultural activism over the last generation, spearheaded by multiple community-based and national nongovernmental organizations (NGOs).

Essential to the pan-Maya movement has been an interest in *reappropriating* (according to Western academia) and *reinterpreting* (from an indigenous perspective) aspects of ancestral and modern Maya culture, including archaeological materials, ethnohistoric documents, hieroglyphic script, numerical and calendric systems, and traditional forms of weaving.[9] Many organizations focus further on the revitalization of institutions and community language, on establishing culturally inclusive education, and on changing official political and civic norms to reflect traditional forms of leadership, including a community council of elders, midwives, and shaman-priests. These efforts to reclaim traditional Maya values and cultural institutions constitute a central organizing principle in the lives of many contemporary Maya people. The importance within pre-Hispanic Maya society of ancestral traditions, particularly reverence for the remains of ancestors themselves, has thus become a defining aspect of Maya cultural activism.

Maya people of Mesoamerica have long made pilgrimages to ancient Maya archaeological sites, despite the breakdown of this tradition in many communities. National laws that defined archaeological remains as belonging to the state, however, forced these pilgrimages underground because they required individuals to clandestinely enter government property and conduct rituals, such as burning incense, which had the potential to inadvertently alter archaeological materials. In recent years, Maya people have begun to assert the legitimacy of their unique claim, as a descendant population, to the ancestral landscape by expressing "ownership" of the pre-Hispanic past in spiritual terms. In 2001, Q'eqchi' Maya neighbors to the Classic-period site of Cancuén in western Guatemala acted under their rights as cultural descendants and spiritual heirs of the landscape, and publicly expressed great concern that excavation at the ruins might disturb Tzuultaq'a, the god of the earth.[10] This deity, responsible for the welfare of the community and the world, and capable of fierce retaliation if not properly worshiped, expressed his disdain for the community by appearing in the form of a female ancestor in the dreams of a woman who had formerly lived in the community. The ancestor spoke to the woman and told her that because the Q'eqchi' living near the ruins were too close to the danger, they could not see how Tzuultaq'a needed them.[11] After intensive consultation between community leaders and spiritual guides belonging to a government organization called the Commission of Sacred Sites, all involved determined that the only option was to appease Tzuultaq'a and the ancestors of the site by conducting the appropriate ceremonies. These ceremonies are now conducted each year before the initiation of archaeological excavation and are perceived to be essential to the prevention of disaster and to the maintenance of health and well-being for those living and working near Cancuén.

While Cancuén exemplifies the Maya's concern for ancestors and ancestral deities and the assertion of traditional rights in their appeasement, Maya peoples throughout the region are undertaking renewed efforts in the ceremonial care of ancestral archaeological sites. During 2006, Maya spiritual leaders in southern Belize requested permission from the government to conduct ritual practices at the Classic-period site of Lubaantun. Since 2000, Guatemala has taken steps to ensure the religious freedom of Maya peoples as expressed in their autonomous relationship with archaeological sites.[12] At protected archaeological sites in Guatemala—such as Tikal and Quirigua—the Ministry of Culture and Sports has sanctioned the construction of ritual spaces designated for the open and free conduct of spiritual ceremonies. Following the creation of these sacred spaces, the Ministry made another concession to the religious needs of Maya spiritual leaders, who believed that the removal of the remains of ceremonies compromised the potency of the ceremony itself. A second space for the disposal of ceremonial materials now accompanies the ritual space at protected Guatemalan archaeological sites.

Other efforts by Maya peoples to reclaim parts of their ancestral landscape have encountered strong opposition before ultimately being resolved in favor of recognizing the rights of Maya descendents over their heritage. One of the most famous Classic-period Maya sites, Copán, has been a source of political contention since 1998. Chortí Maya residents of the Copán Valley of Honduras, the only Maya group remaining in Honduras today, have experienced a level of assimilation that far exceeds that which took place in much of Guatemala, Mexico, and Belize; few Chortí Maya recall the spiritual traditions of their culture and even fewer speak the Chortí Maya language. In recent years, however, Chortí leaders have sought to encourage cultural revitalization and the resurgence of indigenous land rights through the construction of a political organization called the National Indigenous Council of the Maya-Chortí of Honduras (CONIMCHH).[13] These efforts have included two takeovers of the archaeological park of Copán (in 1998 and 2000) to redress wrongs against the indigenous community, such as the assault on former land rights, and to express their desire to channel some of the millions of dollars in entrance fees collected each year by the Honduran Institute of Archaeology and History (IHAH) toward the support of dozens of impoverished descendent Chortí communities (specifically to improve school systems and implement a curriculum that includes instruction in the Chortí Maya language, and to build health-care centers).[14] Despite the volatility of these takeovers, resulting in the death of one indigenous leader and the summoning of the Honduran military to end the takeover in 2000, in 2005 the government granted CONIMCCH (and the local municipality) a portion of the entrance fees collected yearly by IHAH.

Ultimately, the resurgence of interest among Maya peoples in the remains of their ancestors is a slow and uneven process that struggles against centuries of cultural subordination, gross economic inequities, and the more recent redefinition of ancestral Maya ruins as sites of tourism that produce revenue for the state. While the increased recognition of the rights of Maya communities as indigenous peoples has opened up new avenues for the expression of cultural traditions and spirituality that were forced underground in the past, for some groups it is ever more difficult to recall cultural connections to the past that have been lost over time. In many ways Maya communities that experienced the greatest opposition to their assertion of ethnic autonomy found solace in the maintenance of a strong connection to their ancestors through spirituality and oral history. The experience of protracted civil war in Guatemala, for instance, provided the impetus for numerous changes in Guatemalan government and policy that bolstered recognition within Guatemala of its multicultural population. With greater opportunities to maneuver within official spheres, Maya peoples are now better able to voice their sense of entitlement to ancient Maya archaeological sites as the remains of their ancestors and the loci of Maya spirituality.

Despite the weakened link between Maya peoples and their ancestors, Maya culture remains strong. Approximately thirty ethnolinguistic groups in southern Mexico, Guatemala, Belize, and western Honduras continue to identify themselves as indigenous Maya peoples. Maya social practices—language, *traje,* spirituality, oral history and mythology, subsistence farming, and food preparation—resonate strongly among those living in both the lowland and highland regions. Laying claim to the conspicuous and awe-inspiring monuments of pre-Columbian times—still prominent features of this ancestral Maya landscape—the Maya cite a tradition with roots going back two thousand years. In reclaiming their ancestral landscape, Maya peoples ensure their cultural survival as an indigenous community that has been present in the region for millennia.

1. William L. Fash, "Changing Perspectives on Maya Civilization," *Annual Review of Anthropology* 23 (1994): 181–208; Joyce Marcus, "Ancient Maya Political Economy," in *Lowland Maya Civilization in the Eighth Century A.D.: A Symposium at Dumbarton Oaks,* October 7–8, 1989, J.A. Sabloff and J.S. Henderson, eds. (Washington, D.C.: Dumbarton Oaks Research Library and Collection, 1993) 111–184; Simon Martin and Nikolai Grube, *Chronicle of the Maya Kings and Queens: Deciphering the Dynasties of the Ancient Maya* (London: Thames & Hudson, 2000); Joel W. Palka, "Sociopolitical Implications of a New Emblem Glyph and Place Name in Maya Inscriptions," *Latin American Antiquity* 7, no. 3 (1996): 211–227.
2. Gary H. Gossen and Richard M. Leventhal, "The Topography of Ancient Maya Religious Pluralism: A Dialogue with the Present," in *Lowland Maya Civilization in the Eighth Century, A.D., A Symposium at Dumbarton Oaks,* October 7–8, 1989, J.A. Sabloff and J.S. Henderson, eds. (Washington, D.C.: Dumbarton Oaks Research Library and Collection, 1993) 185–218.
3. Patricia A. McAnany, *Living with the Ancestors: Kinship and Kingship in Ancient Maya Society* (Austin: University of Texas Press, 1995).
4. Ellen E. Bell, "Engendering a Dynasty: A Royal Woman in the Margarita Tomb, Copan," in *Ancient Maya Women,* T. Ardren, ed. (Walnut Creek, CA: AltaMira Press, 2002), 89–104.

5. Bruce G. Trigger, "Alternative Archaeologies: Nationalist, Colonialist, Imperialist," *Man* 19, no. 3 (1984): 355–370.

6. Demetrio Cojti Cuxil (Waqi' Q'anil), *Configuración del Pensamiento Político del Pueblo Maya (2da. Parte)* (Guatemala City: Editorial CHOLSAMAJ, 1995), 102; Demetrio Cojti Cuxil (Waqi' Q'anil), "The Politics of Maya Revindication," in *Maya Cultural Activism in Guatemala*, E. F. Fischer and R. M. Brown, eds. (Austin: University of Texas Press, 1996) 33; Edward F. Fischer and R. McKenna Brown, "Introduction: Maya Cultural Activism in Guatemala," in *Maya Cultural Activism in Guatemala*, Fischer and Brown, eds. (Austin: University of Texas Press, 1996) 9.

7. Faye V. Harrison, "Anthropology as an Agent of Transformation: Introductory Comments and Queries," in *Decolonizing Anthropology: Moving Further toward an Anthropology for Liberation,* F. V. Harrison, ed. (Arlington, VA: American Anthropological Association, 1991), 1–15.

8. Benedict Anderson, *Imagined Communities: Reflections on the Origin and Spread of Nationalism* (London: Verso, 1991).

9. Edward F. Fischer, "Induced Culture Change as a Strategy for Socioeconomic Development: The Pan-Maya Movement in Guatemala," Fischer and Brown, eds. (Austin: University of Texas Press, 1996) 64–65.

10. David Ricardo García Alfaro, *Los Mayas en Cancuén: Ideología y Religión alrededor de un Proyecto Arqueológico.* Licenciatura Thesis (Guatemala City: Universidad del Valle de Guatemala, 2003), 96–100.

11. Ibid., 110–120.

12. Ministry of Culture and Sports, Guatemala, 2005. "Unidad de Lugares Sagrados," published online at http://www.mcd.gob.gt/MICUDE/el_ministerio/direccion_patrimonio/lugares_sagrados. Accessed April 20, 2006.

13. Lena Michaela Mortensen, *Constructing Heritage at Copan, Honduras: An Ethnography of the Archaeology Industry.* PhD Dissertation (Bloomington, IN: Indiana University, 2005).

14. Ibid., 258–277.

THEIR VISION PASSED BEYOND THE MOUNTAINS: THE MAYA AND DIVINE SIGHT

by Allen J. Christenson

Bruce Martin's ethereal photograph (page 121) of a maize plant would be an appropriate starting point to explore the way the Maya view the world. Traditionalist Maya eat maize at every meal, mirroring a practice among their ancient ancestors that goes back thousands of years. For the Maya people, maize is far more than just food. It is the sacred flesh of their principal god who created the world. Grains of maize are treated with great respect in Maya households. If several grains should fall to the floor accidentally, or if a young child unknowingly should spill some, the mother of the household will often stop whatever she is doing, tenderly pick up the maize, dust it off and apologize for not showing it the proper honor. Most Maya love to talk and laugh, but in traditional households there is little talking during mealtimes. For most, this is just the way things have always been done. They grew up not speaking during meals, so they carry on the custom. But older people, who tend to think more about such things, know that the silence is a matter of respect. A highly respected K'iche'-Maya priest once told me:

> When I was young my father told me that when we eat our tortillas and tamalitos we are eating something sacred. It is the body of God. The Catholics, when they go to Mass, say they are eating the flesh of God when they eat the Host of the sacrament. They do this once a week. The Host is made of wheat, and their God is a wheat God. For us, maize is our God; he is the one who made us. We are maize people. We eat his flesh at every meal and therefore our bodies are made of maize. One doesn't play with such things. To eat maize is sacred to us. One doesn't talk at such times or gossip. If we did, our ancestors

27

would punish us for not showing proper respect. Young people sometimes forget this. But it is very dangerous.

Partly because of this belief, the K'iche'-Maya see themselves as *qas winaq* ("true people"). This is not to say that wheat people, or rye people, or Kentucky Fried Chicken people are not perfectly fine people in their way, but they are qualitatively different. Their flesh is not composed of Maya maize and therefore they do not have Maya blood in their veins; they do not "remember" the thoughts and traditions of their ancestors because these are inherent in the flesh of maize, which is common to all Maya people who partake of it. Maize is not just food; it is sacred memory—it is what makes the Maya who and what they are. It used to be that this maize had to be locally grown maize. Families would sometimes go hungry when their stores of local maize had run out, even if they could have purchased maize from nearby communities. "That is their maize, not ours," the prevailing wisdom holds. I once asked a Maya woman in Momostenango why that should matter and she told me, "That maize comes from their ancestors. It is different. We would be different if we ate it."

While working in Maya communities in the 1970s doing linguistic and ethnographic research, it generally took me about nine months to learn one of the many Maya languages well enough to carry on a good conversation. I happened to mention this to one of my Maya friends, who good-naturedly suggested that this was because in nine months I had eaten Maya food long enough that my body had been "reconstructed" as a Maya. Just as it takes nine months to form a child in the womb, it takes nine months to re-create a human being by eating maize. If I hadn't been eating maize all that time, that is, I couldn't have spoken Maya.

According to the *Popol Vuh*, a K'iche'-Maya text compiled in the highlands of Guatemala soon after the Spanish Conquest in the sixteenth century, the first Maya men were formed by maize, ground nine times by the moon goddess Xmucane:

> Thus was found the food that would become the flesh of the newly framed and shaped people. Water was their blood. It became the blood of humanity. The ears of maize entered into their flesh by means of She Who Has Borne Children and He

Who Has Begotten Sons. . . . The yellow ears of maize and the white ears of maize were then ground fine with nine grindings by Xmucane. Food entered their flesh, along with water to give them strength. . . . Thus their frame and shape were given expression by our first Mother and our first Father. Their flesh was merely yellow ears of maize and white ears of maize. Mere food were the legs and arms of humanity, of our first fathers.[1]

These "maize people" were the culmination of various failed attempts at creating beings who would "remember" the gods who had created them and who would carry out the proper rituals and prayers to perpetuate the universe. Maya religion is an immanent one, meaning that the gods are not distant, unapproachable beings. Sacred beings are everywhere—in the mountains, the rivers, the rain, and particularly within the Maya themselves. For the ancient Maya, the principal god of creation was the Maize God, who, through the sacrifice and offering of his own flesh, was able to create human beings in his youthful, beautiful appearance. He is often depicted on ceramic vessels or carved stone monuments dancing the world into creation, carrying the makings of the sky, earth, and all living things as a burden on his back. Each time a Maya farmer plants his maize, tends it, and harvests it, he is re-creating the means by which the world is reborn. In the *Popol Vuh,* human beings are called "the provider, the strengthener, the sustainer." Without them, the creator gods declare that there can be no "first planting," no "dawn of the sun."[2] Maize is in many ways a human creation. It has been cultivated for thousands of years by the Maya to look the way it does. There is no such thing as wild maize. Because its ears are enveloped in a thick husk, its seeds cannot be released without human intervention. If no one planted maize one year, maize would cease to be. The Maya recognize this and see themselves as mediators, standing with one foot in this world and one in the world of the sacred. Without them, the gods would vanish and all creation would slip back into the darkness and chaos that existed before the first dawn. For this reason, the Maya take their responsibilities to recite proper prayers and perform sacred rituals very seriously. Literally, the world depends on it.

According to the *Popol Vuh,* the first ancestors, made of maize, had the gift of extraordinary vision whereby they could see all things:

Perfect was their sight, and perfect was their knowledge of everything beneath the sky. If they gazed about them, turning their faces around, they beheld that which was in the sky and that which was upon the earth. Instantly, they were able to behold everything. They didn't have to walk to see all that existed beneath the sky. They merely saw it from wherever they were. Thus their knowledge became full. Their vision passed beyond the trees and rocks, beyond the lakes and the seas, beyond the mountains and the valleys.[3]

The ancestors of the K'iche'-Maya were described also in the *Titulo Totonicapán* as being magical and wise people whose sight reached far into the sky and the earth; there was nothing to equal all that they could "see" beneath the sky.[4] Although the creator gods eventually clouded this vision so that men could only see those things that were "nearby,"[5] the progenitors of the Maya and their descendants nevertheless bore within their blood the potential for divine sight, bestowed upon them by their creators. Present-day *ajq'ijab'* (daykeepers, or priests who continue traditional Maya religious practices) believe that their divine ancestors, who set the pattern for contemporary rituals, continue to operate through them as conduits at certain times and under particular circumstances. It is their sacred ancestral vision that allows the *ajq'ij* to "see" beyond the limits of time and distance as the first men once did. Evon Vogt noted that the Tzotzil-Maya of Zinacantán believe that in ancient times their people could see inside sacred mountains where the ancestors live. Today only shamans are recognized as having this ability. Thus, the Tzotzil term *h'ilol* means "seer," in the sense of one who can "see" things on a supernatural level.[6]

Among the Maya, there is no institutional religion to sanction the qualification of a person to become an *ajq'ij*. All Maya men and women potentially have this ability because it is inherent in their blood. *Ajq'ijab'* are chosen by the ancestors to serve as mediators between this world and the spirit world, not because they are qualitatively different from anyone else in this regard, but because they are called by the spirit world to do so on behalf of their community. The Maya refer to this as their *burden,* the same word they use to refer to the heavy burdens men carry on their backs, secured by a forehead strap, when traveling long distances. Once called, generally through dreams or the discovery of a sign interpreted as an invitation to serve from the ancestors, the prospective *ajq'ij* often enters a period of apprenticeship. Experienced *ajq'ijab'* train their apprentices to interpret signs and spirit communications, described as "lightning in the blood," which they had always received since young childhood but lacked the experience to understand properly. Thus Bunzel noted that *ajq'ijab'* have no special relationship with divinity, and their prayers, though perhaps more eloquent, are no more efficacious than those voiced by commoners.[7]

For this reason, not all *ajq'ijab'* go through a process of apprenticeship. A well-respected *ajq'ij*, named Diego, living in the Tz'utujil-Maya community of Santiago Atitlán, told me that although he had watched a number of elderly *ajq'ijab'* carry out prayers and ceremonies in his youth, he did not learn how to do his work from them:

> When I was born, I already knew how to do these things. I had no teacher. I speak with the ancestors and ancient kings and they speak with me. They help me to know how to heal and solve problems for people. I ask the ancestors these things in places that are holy, where I can be touched by them.

Mendelson was told by an *ajkun* (a "healer," the most prevalent type of traditional priest in Santiago Atitlán) that sacred knowledge cannot be passed from one person to another. It must come from deity:

> He said that a young man who wished to be an *ajkun* tried to learn the prayers, bit by bit, from another *ajkun* but that there were no direct courses of lessons given by an old man to a pupil and that there could not be since these things came from God. For this reason each *ajkun* had a different way of praying.[8]

Apprenticeships and learning by example are undoubtedly important methods of passing along knowledge from one generation to the next; however, the Maya *ajq'ijab'* believe that this is not the principal means by which sacred knowledge is acquired. This must come directly from within themselves, directly from their own blood, or it is powerless. Non-Maya do not necessarily have this kind of ability, because their blood does not originate from the same visionary ancestral source. In my own experience working with *ajq'ijab'* in Momostenango in the late 1970s, my frequent displays of ineptitude in learning divinatory and calendric skills were interpreted as stemming from the lack of Maya blood in my veins. I was not able to see with ancestral vision in the same way because I had a different lineage, likely not a very divine one.

Bunzel noted that the K'iche' of Chichicastenango claimed that their formalized speech and ceremonies were attributed to ancient ancestral precedent: "And now this rite and custom belongs to the first people, our mothers and fathers. . . . This belongs to them; we are the embodiment of their rites and ceremonies."[9] To alter the actions of the ancestors would be to change the very fabric of their existence in potentially destructive ways. As mediators between this world and that of the sacred, it is the Maya's obligation to carry out the mandates of their divine ancestors in as authentic a manner as possible. As one of them noted: "It is our name and destiny to repeat and perpetuate these ceremonies before the world."[10] When asking Tz'utujils when certain rituals began, a common response is that they are as old as the world and were first performed by their ancestors who had divine power.[11, 12]

At the beginning of ritual prayers, *ajq'ijab'* and *ajkuns* in Santiago Atitlán, Guatemala, call upon a litany of sacred beings and objects whose power they wish to invoke on behalf of their clients. Prominent in this list are ancestors and ancient Maya rulers. One year, during Easter Week, I went with an *ajq'ij* in Santiago Atitlán to conduct a ceremony on the ruins of the ancient Tz'utujil capital of Chutinamit. He chose this location because there he was "closer to the kings of old and therefore sacred." Prior to the ceremony he selected twelve flat stones and arranged them into a rough square, which he called his "table," before laying out a clean cloth and arranging his ritual paraphernalia for the ceremony. He said that the makeshift altar had the same power as the tables and/or altars on which sacred objects are kept in his home, or in the town's church, or in the various confraternity houses in town. He placed four lit cigars on the north side of this temporary table so that the ancestors who were called to be present at the ceremony could smoke and be content.

The four corners of a shamanic table's surface represent the four corners of the world, and the placement of objects upon it suggests the arrangement of specific locations on the earth, such as mountains or shrines. The table thus circumscribes the sacred geography of the universe in a form that becomes intimate, close, and potentially manipulable. One of Bruce Martin's photos (page 106) shows a ritual altar or table with offerings on it. Vogt quoted a highland Maya man from Zinacantán as saying that the universe is "like a house, like a table," representing that which is systematic, and well-ordered.[13] Charles Wisdom also recorded that the Chortí-Maya of Guatemala considered both the squared maize field and the shamanic altar as the world in miniature.[14] By laying out the maize field, or setting up a ritual altar, the Maya transform secular places into sacred space. With regard to the maize field, this charges the ground with the power of creation to bear new life. In a similar way, the altar provides a stage on which sacred geography may be intimately studied, and even altered. As Mary Helms writes, "to re-create cosmic harmony and governance [is] ultimately to strive to control such powers and to apply them to human affairs."[15] Ancient Maya altars served the same function, and were often carved with ancestral figures—gods and symbols that represent the life-generating powers of the world.

In addition to being one of the world's oldest living cultures, the Maya of today are also a modern people. They are not a lost civilization somehow rediscovered from the ancient past. And like any living society, they are well aware of the world beyond the borders of their communities and readily adopt aspects of non-Maya culture, art, and language that fit the ever-changing needs of their people. Soon after the Spanish Conquest, missionary priests actively replaced the images of native gods with those of European Christian saints. But, in the eyes of the Maya, these Christian icons acquired the powers and status of the older pre-Columbian deities. Thomas Gage, who visited Guatemala in the 1630s, wrote that the Maya devoutly worshiped the Christian saints "because they look upon them as much like unto their forefathers' idols. The churches are full of them."[16] The saints in Bruce Martin's photographs are common throughout the Maya world. In the early colonial-era church at Santiago Atitlán, rows of saints line the sides of the nave. At sunset, these saints cast red shadows against the wall, an effect produced by the setting sun shining through a red stained-glass window. The Tz'utujil-Maya of the community love this effect, describing the shadows as the blood or sacrifice of the saints. It is this sacrifice that fills the world with new life, much as the sacrifice of the Maize God bestows new life.

A traditionalist Atiteco named Nicolás Chavez Sojuel told me that when the Spaniards came the earth died along with all the ancient gods and kings. But he went on to point out that the earth has died many times. Each time the world and its gods are reborn to new life, they regain their former power. Thus Nicolás explained that the saints today have Spanish names because the old earth died in the days of the Spanish conquerors: "When the spirit keepers of the world appeared again they were the saints, but they do the same work that the old gods did in ancient times."

Mendelson noted that the Tz'utujils celebrate the death and rebirth of their old gods in the history of the Christian God.[17] This is not because the Maya perceive their ancient gods as equivalent in all respects with Christ and the saints, but because each set of deities perform similar roles in society. It is these similarities that Tz'utujils choose to emphasize, rather than the differences. Atitecos seldom consider whether the components of a myth or ritual are Christian or Maya. It is simply the religion that has existed since the beginning of time as ordained by all the gods and saints, including Martín, Santiago, Christ, and others. These practices must be continued according to the patterns set by the Tz'utujil ancestors or the world will die.

It is the ability of the Maya to change while maintaining their identity that characterizes much of the history of Santiago Atitlán. The Tz'utujil-Maya adapt to their changing world by interpreting those changes in uniquely Maya ways. A young traditionalist Maya priest told me, "As the old people say, when the Spaniards came they broke off many of our branches. They even burned the trunk. But we will never die because the roots have power. We draw strength from the ancestors who live in our blood. If we as a people ignore our roots, we will all die."

The Maya do not abandon their identity as Maya in accepting elements of foreign ideas in their worship. Nor are these Christian elements just a superficial gilding of Roman Catholicism to hide the "true" Maya nature. The Maya have incorporated new influences for thousands of years, from Olmec beginnings, to Teotihuacan, to so-called "Toltec" influences, to cultural exchanges from contact with the Mexica of central Mexico. The Maya of today, particularly in Santiago Atitlán, have succeeded in incorporating much of the technology of the twenty-first century—such as cellular phones, computers, and cable television—into their lives while maintaining their identity as Maya.

34

Their devotion to traditional dress, language, and identity is a source of great comfort and strength in the face of a modern world that is changing rapidly and often cruel.

1. Allen J. Christenson, *Popol Vuh: The Sacred Book of the Maya* (Winchester, UK, and New York: O Books, 2003), 194–95.
2. Ibid., 200.
3. Ibid., 197–98.
4. Robert M. Carmack and James L. Mondloch, *El Título de Totonicapán* (México: Universidad Nacional Autónoma de México, 1983), 71. English translation by Christenson.
5. Christenson, 201.
6. Evon Z. Vogt, *Tortillas for the Gods: A Symbolic Analysis of Zinacanteco Rituals* (Norman: University of Oklahoma Press, 1993), 205.
7. Ruth Bunzel, *Chichicastenango: A Guatemalan Village* (Seattle: University of Washington Press, 1952), 299.
8. E. Michael Mendelson, *Religion and World-View in a Guatemalan Village*, Microfilm Collection of Manuscripts on Middle American Cultural Anthropology, no. 52 (Chicago: University of Chicago Library, 1957), 280–81.
9. Bunzel, 232, 238.
10. Ibid., 242.
11. Allen J. Christenson, *Art and Society in a Highland Maya Community: The Altarpiece of Santiago Atitlán* (Austin: University of Texas Press, 2000), 22–23, 68.
12. E. Michael Mendelson, *Los escándalos de Maximon*, Seminario de Integración Social Guatemalteca, Publication 19 (Guatemala City: Tipografía Nacional, 1965), 91.
13. Vogt, 11.
14. Charles Wisdom, *Chorti Indians of Guatemala* (Chicago: University of Chicago Press, 1940), 430.
15. Mary W. Helms, *Craft and the Kingly Ideal: Art, Trade, and Power* (Austin: University of Texas Press, 1993), 27.
16. Thomas Gage, *Thomas Gage's Travels in the New World*, J. Eric S. Thompson, ed. (Norman: University of Oklahoma Press, 1958), 234–35.
17. Mendelson, *Los escándalos*, 138.

PLATES

The Maya, a group of Central American Indians, live today in Belize, El Salvador, Guatemala, Honduras, and Southern Mexico. Their rich history and traditions offer a unique and interesting perspective on life and its foundations.

Over five million people, comprising at least thirty distinct ethnolinguistic groups, are descended from the Maya who inhabited great and complex civilizations throughout Central America for over two thousand years before the arrival of Spanish conquistadors in the sixteenth century.

Milpa Farmer, Maní, Yucatán, Mexico, 1996

*Zunil, Western Highlands,
Guatemala, 1999*

Opchen, Yucatán, Mexico, 1994

ABOVE LEFT, RIGHT, AND OPPOSITE: *Todos Santos, Cuchumatan, Guatemala, 1999*

ABOVE LEFT, RIGHT, AND OPPOSITE LEFT, RIGHT: *Maní, Yucatán, Mexico, 1996*

Maya civilization has undergone many transformations since its origins in the pre-Classic period, ca. 1200 BC–AD 250.

From an adjacent culture, the Olmecs, the pre-Classic Maya borrowed and adapted a written language, a complex calendar, and a complicated world view. To solidify their Maya identity and confirm their beliefs, they developed large scale building projects, a complex cosmology, and elaborate rituals that employed a sophisticated iconographic system.

The most recognizable archaeological sites of Maya cities
and ceremonial structures were built during the Classic
era, ca. 250–800 A.D.

Tikal, El Petén, Guatemala, 1990

The pyramids were manmade mountains with aspects of caves. Built by the Classic-era Maya communities to serve both bureaucratic and religious purposes, they mapped out sacred space on earth. Their construction created the opportunity for the elites to controllarge groups of laborers and many community resources.

El Castillo, Xunantunich, Cayo District, Belize, 1998

Caves, natural entrances to the invisible world, are considered places of great power and mystery. Often, they are associated with divine beings, weather activity, diseases, birth, and corn.

Loltun Cave, Yucatán, Mexico, 1994

Rio Frio Cave, Cayo District, Belize, 1998

Chicanná, Campeche, Mexico, 1994

Altun Ha, Belize District, Belize, 1991   **57**

Yaxchilán, Chiapas, Mexico, 1990

Dos Pilas, El Petén, Guatemala, 1991

Santa Lucia Cotzumalguapa,
Escuintla Department, Guatemala,
1989

".... of the monuments themselves, standing as they
do in depths of a tropical forest, silent and solemn,
strange in design, excellent in sculpture, rich in orna-
ment, different from the works of any other people,
their whole history so entirely unknown, with hieroglyphics explaining all, but perfectly unintelligible . . . "

—John L. Stephens, *Incidents of Travel in
Central America, Chiapas and Yucatán*
(New York: Dover Publications, 1969; first
published by Harper & Brothers, 1841)

Quirigua, Izabal Department, Guatemala, 1989

Kohunlich, Quintana Roo, Mexico, 1994

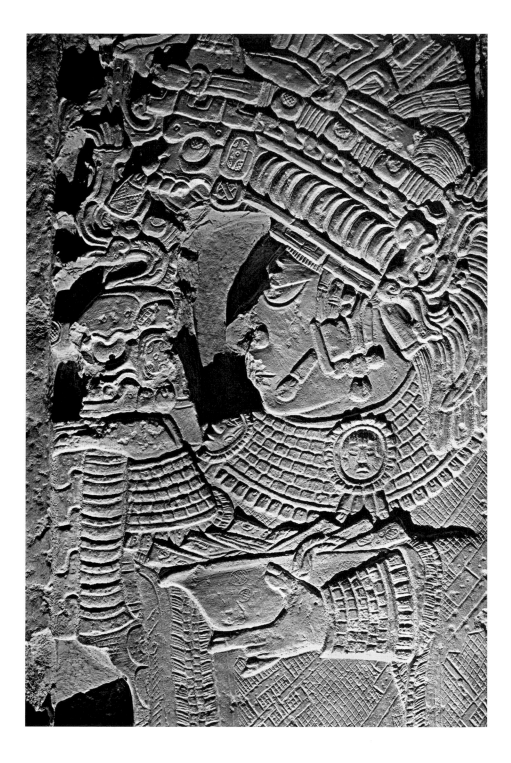

Yaxchilán, Chiapas, Mexico, 1990

The tropical forest is important to the Maya as a physical
resource and as a sacred guide for spiritual renewal.
Today, the Central American rainforest is disappearing
at an epidemic rate of over 700,000 acres per year,
according to the Food and Agriculture Organization
of the United Nations.

Big Rock Falls, Mountain Pine Ridge, Cayo District,
Belize, 1998

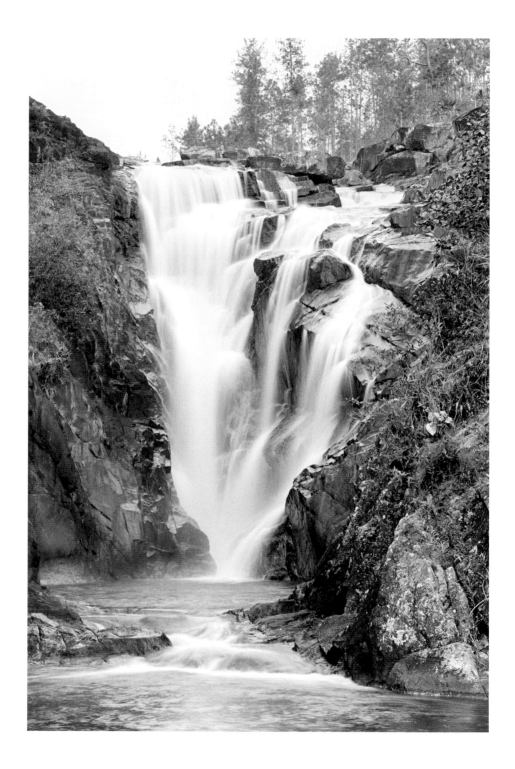

Aguateca, El Petén, Guatemala, 1993

Dos Pilas, El Petén, Guatemala, 1991

Altar de Sacrificios, Rio La Pasión, El Petén, Guatemala, 1993

Dos Pilas, El Petén, Guatemala, 1991

Dos Pilas, El Petén, Guatemala, 1993

Ruins throughout the Maya region are records of the ancestral accomplishments, practices, and beliefs. Often buried or merging with the lush forest background, they bear witness to an era of Maya civilization that might otherwise be lost to time.

Piedras Negras, Rio Usumacinta, El Petén, Guatemala, 2001

Topoxte, El Petén, Guatemala, 2001

Tikal, El Petén, Guatemala, 1989

TOP RIGHT: *El Ceibal, Rio La Pasión,*
El Petén, Guatemala, 1991

BOTTOM RIGHT: *Itzan, El Petén,*
Guatemala, 1993

Topoxte, El Petén, Guatemala, 2001

*Piedras Negras, Rio Usumacinta, El
Petén, Guatemala, 2001*

Arroyo de Piedras, El Petén,
Guatemala, 1993

Stela 2, Dos Pilas, El Petén, Guatemala, 1991

Weathered faces, elaborate dress, and writings abound
throughout Maya sites on limestone sculptures. The
images incised into stone tell of the history and partici-
pants of these ceremonial centers. They reflect the Maya
idea that reality is a series of layers with sacred energies
lying behind all objects and outward appearances.

Stela 9 states:
It was on 7 ahau 3 pop, the tree stone of time ended (AD 625)
It was 6 Kib 4 Zec then 17 yrs 4 days earlier (AD 608),
in his sacred place, he became ruler
He is the younger son of the previous ruler
His name is Snail Shell That Smokes, Lord Smoking Shell
His celestial Progenitor is the Spirit Crocodile
Lord east of the province of LAMA'AN'AIN

Stela 9, Lamanai, Orange Walk District, Belize, 1998

Maya remains and present attitudes tell of a culture consumed with understanding the rhythms of nature, reality, and time. They show a desire to synchronize with these primal forces, so that the flow of their life can continue.

At Yaxchilán, on the edge of partially cleared areas, small structures sit on broken stairways that disappear at the bottom of the mound into the jungle. Many structures appear as fragments with two or three doorways that lead to open stands of trees.

Once part of a larger complex that covered the entire platform, they are now small islands of cut stone in a sea of green.

Yaxchilán, Chiapas, Mexico, 1990

*Sayil, Puuc Region, Yucatán, Mexico,
1987*

Sayil, Puuc Region, Yucatán, Mexico, 1987 **91**

Chacmultun, Yucatán, Mexico, 1996

Labna, Puuc Region, Yucatán, Mexico, 1987

Sayil, Puuc Region, Yucatán, Mexico, 1987   **95**

Diego de Landa, a Catholic Friar, traveled throughout the Yucatán in the 1500s and later became the region's bishop. He is a key figure in understanding the collision of the Spanish and Maya cultures. To help in his conversion of natives to Christianity, he learned their language, customs and religion. His book, *Relación de las Cosas de Yucatán,* is an important and early source on these subjects. Ironically, this book was written as part of his defense in Spanish Court for his cruel and excessive treatment of Maya under his control.

Image of Bishop Diego de Landa, Izamal, Yucatán, Mexico, 1994

Throughout history, outside groups have introduced new symbols into the Maya's belief system. The Maya have, until recently, been able to keep their core symbols by covering them with the visual structures of the new icons.

Church altar, Maní, Yucatán, Mexico, 1996

In a hillside village overlooking Lake Atitlán, in the highlands of southern Guatemala, a new member is joining the sect of San Simon. San Simon connects the physical world to the unseen world. With offerings and prayers, his caretakers keep San Simon alive so he can fulfill his followers' desires.

Santiago Atitlán, Lake Atitlán, Guatemala, 1999

Santiago Atitlán, Lake Atitlán, Guatemala, 1999

San Andres Itzapa, Chimaltenango Department,
Guatemala, 1999

A home altar prepared for All Saints Day. The food,
a symbolic payment by the living to the dead, will be
spiritually eaten by the ancestors, then physically eaten
by their living descendents.

Maní, Yucatán, Mexico, 1996

Chichicastengo, Guatemala, 1992

Maní, Yucatán, Mexico, 1996

Maní, Yucatán, Mexico, 1996

San Jose altar, Maní, Yucatán, Mexico, 1996

Maní, Yucatán, Mexico, 1996

In western Honduras lies a valley carved out by the Rio Copán. The valley, once populated by the Chortí Maya, is now home to their descendants and a mix of settlers that have come into the area over the years.

"... In this matter, we together gained knowledge of magic science, and of greatness and power. We humbled ourselves before the fathers and grandfathers of us. And the glory of the birth of our early fathers was never extinguished ... "

> —*The Annals of the Cakchiquels,* translated by Adrian Recinos, and Delia Goetz (Norman, OK: University of Oklahoma Press, 1953)

Copán, Honduras, 1989

Gone now is the tropical forest that once hid the Ruinas de Copán from intruders. What remain in this fertile valley are some of the best examples of Classic Maya sculpture and structures to be seen today. Here, the stone carvings break away from the flat relief carvings of most other Maya sites into a full, rounded style that reflects both the inspiring environment and iconography the Maya so cherished.

LEFT AND OPPOSITE:
Copán, Honduras, 1992

Farming is the main source of income in the valley, with the well-known "trinity" of corn, beans, and squash leading the way. A variety of other crops such as bananas, tomatoes, and radishes, are grown in the rich land along the river, in addition to the income producing crops of coffee, cotton, and tobacco.

Copán, Honduras, 1992

One of the defining symbols of the Maya is corn. Far more than just a primary source of food, corn reflects the cycle of life and embodies the essence of the god who created the world.

Calcehtok, Yucatán, Mexico, 1996

Subsistence farming provides a limited amount of food to support a family. Good harvests can produce extra food for barter, but a poor one can leave the family undernourished and destitute.

LEFT AND OPPOSITE:
Uaxactun, El Petén, Guatemala, 2001

Quintana Roo, Mexico, 1994

Mul Chic, Yucatán, Mexico, 1996

Traditional farming methods, such as slash and burn, are still used thoughout the region. This is a low cost way to fertilize land but exacerbates soil erosion, the greenhouse effect, and deforestation.

130   *Copán, Honduras, 1992*

Western Highlands, Guatemala, 1993   **131**

Inadequate health care and education have led to high rates of illiteracy, infant mortality, and poverty all over the region.

The Mopan Maya of southern Belize have lost their community's memory of their past and become disconnected from their heritage.

Uxbenka, Toledo District, Belize, 1998

LEFT AND OPPOSITE:
Uxbenka, Toledo District, Belize,
1998

Many contemporary Maya continue to respect traditional viewpoints. They remember their past and continue to practice many long-established activities in their daily life. At the same time, children are leaving behind this world and losing touch with their cultural identity.

Milpa farmer, Maní, Yucatán, Mexico, 1996

ABOVE AND OPPOSITE: *Tixacal Guardia, Quintana Roo, Mexico, 1994*

The Maya speak from their hearts in discussing the problems they confront, yet they have little political clout with which to improve their situation. Surviving the twenty-first century will be the greatest challenge the Maya culture has ever faced.

Milpa Farmer, Mul Chic, Yucatán, Mexico, 1991

FOLLOWING SPREAD: *Lake Yaxha, El Petén, Guatemala, 2001*

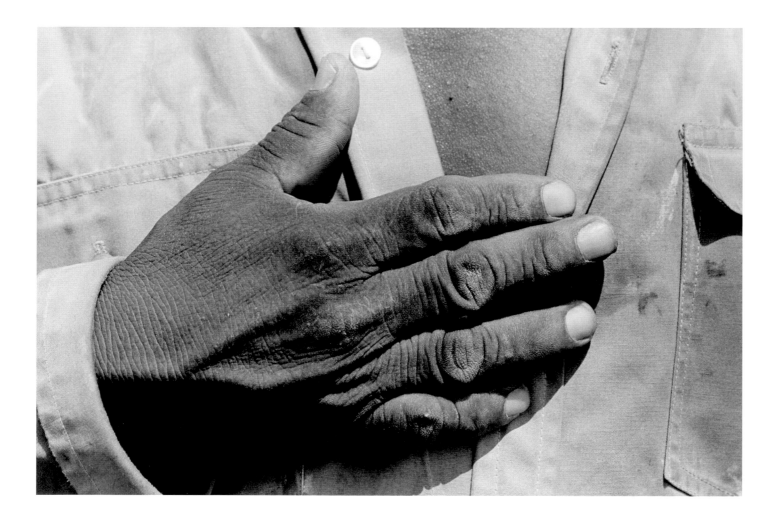

BIBLIOGRAPHY AND SUGGESTED READING

Arvigo, Rosita. *Sastun*. San Francisco: Harper San Francisco, 1992.

Aveni, Anthony F., ed. *The Sky in Mayan Literature*. New York and Oxford: Oxford University Press, 1992.

Bassie-Sweet, Karen. *From the Mouth of the Dark Cave*. Norman, OK: University of Oklahoma Press, 1991.

Baudez, Claude, and Sydney Picasso. *Lost Cities of the Maya*. 1st ed. New York: Harry N. Abrams, Inc., 1992.

Benson, Elizabeth P. and Gillett G. Griffin. *Maya Iconography*. Princeton: Princeton University Press, 1988.

Bricker, Victoria Reifler. *The Indian Christ, the Indian King: The Historical Substrate of Maya Myth and Ritual*. Austin: Univeristy of Texas Press, 1981.

Burns, Allan F., trans. *An Epoch of Miracles*. 1st ed. Austin: University of Texas Press, 1983.

Christenson, Allen J. *Art and Society in a Highland Maya Community*. Austin: University of Texas Press, 2001.

Clendinnen, Inga. *Ambivalent Conquests*. Cambridge: Cambridge University Press, 1987.

Coe, Michael D. *Breaking the Maya Code*. New York: Thames and Hudson, 1992.

———. *The Maya*. 4th ed. New York: Thames and Hudson, 1984.

Collier, John, Jr., and Malcolm Collier. *Visual Anthropology*. Albuquerque: University of New Mexico Press, 1986.

Danien, Elin C., and Robert J. Sharer, eds. *New Theories on the Ancient Maya*. Philadelphia: University of Pennsylvania Museum Publication, 1992.

Davies, Nigel. *The Ancient Kingdoms of Mexico*. New York: Penguin Books, 1982.

Demarest, Arthur A., and Geoffery W. Conrad, eds. *Ideology and Pre Columbian Civilizations*. Santa Fe: SAR Press, 1992.

Desmond, Lawrence Gustave, and Phyllis Mauch Messenger. *A Dream of Maya*. Albuquerque: University of New Mexico Press, 1988.

Díaz, Bernal. *The Conquest of New Spain*. Translated by J.M. Cohen. London: Penguin Group, 1963.

Drew, David. *The Lost Chronicles of the Maya Kings*. Berkeley: University of California Press, 1999.

Edmonson, Munro S. *Heaven Born Merida and Its Destiny: The Book of Chilam Balam of Chumayel*. Austin: University of Texas Press, 1986.

Edwards, Elizabeth, ed. *Anthropology & Photography:1860~1920*. New Haven: Yale University Press, 1992.

Farriss, Nancy M. *Maya Society Under Colonial Rule*. Princeton: Princeton University Press, 1984.

Fash, William L. *Scribes, Warriors and Kings: The City of Copán and the Ancient Maya*. London: Thames and Hudson, 1991.

Freidel, David, Linda Schele, and Joy Parker. *Maya Cosmos: Three Thousand Years on the Shaman's Path*. New York: William Morrow and Company, Inc., 1993.

Goetz, Delia, and Sylvanus Griswold Morley. *The Book of the People: Popol Vuh*. Los Angeles: The Plantin Press, 1954.

———. *Popul Vuh: The Sacred Book of the Ancient Quiché Maya*. Norman, OK: University of Oklahoma Press, 1950.

Hammond, Norman. *Ancient Maya Civilizations*. 3rd ed. New Brunswick, NJ: Rutgers University Press, 1988.

Henderson, John S. *The World of the Ancient Maya*. Ithaca, NY: Cornell University Press, 1981.

Heyden, Doris and Paul Gendrop. *Pre-Columbian Architecture of Mesoamerica*. Translated by Judith Stanton. Milan: Electa S.pA., 1973.

Ingham, John M. *Mary, Michael, and Lucifer: Folk Catholicism in Central Mexico*. Austin: University of Texas Press, 1986.

King, Jaime Litvak. *Ancient Mexico: An Overview*. Albuquerque: University of New Mexico Press, 1985.

Landa, Diego de. *Relacion de los Cosas de Yucatan*. Translated by Alfred M. Tozzer. Cambridge, MA: Peabody Museum Papers, Harvard University, 1941.

Laughlin, Robert M. trans., and Carol Karasik, ed. *The People of the Bat: Mayan Tales and Dreams from Zinacantán*. Washington, DC: Smithsonian Institution Press, 1988.

Léon-Portilla, Miguel. *Time and Reality in the Thought of the Maya*. 2nd ed. Norman, OK: University of Oklahoma Press, 1988.

Love, Bruce. *The Paris Codex: Handbook for a Maya Priest*. Austin: University of Texas Press, 1994.

Makemson, Maud Worcester. *The Book of the Jaguar Priest*. New York: Henry Schuman, 1951.

Marcus, Joyce. *Mesoamerican Writing System*. Princeton: Princeton University Press, 1992.

McAnany, Patricia A. *Living with the Ancestors: Kinship and Kingship in Ancient Maya Society*. Austin: University of Texas Press, 1995.

Montejo, Victor. *The Bird Who Cleans the World and other Mayan Fables*. Translated by Wallace Kaufman. Willimantic, CT: Curbstone Press, 1991.

Morley, Sylvanus G., George W. Brainerd, and Robert J. Sharer. *The Ancient Maya*. Palo Alto, CA: Stanford University Press, 1983.

Morris, Walter F., Jr. *Living Maya*. New York: Harry N. Abrams, Inc., 1987.

Peacock, James L. *The Anthropological Lens: Harsh Lights, Soft Focus*. Cambridge: Cambridge University Press, 1994.

Pearce, Kenneth. *The View from the Top of the Temple*. Albuquerque: University of New Mexico Press, 1984.

Peissel, Michel. *The Lost World of Quintana Roo*. New York: E.P. Dutton & Co., Inc., 1963.

Perara, Victor, and Robert D. Bruce. *The Last Lords of Palenque: The Lacandon Mayas of the Mexican Rain Forest*. Berkeley: University of California Press, 1982.

Perry, Richard, and Rosalind Perry. *Maya Missions: Exploring the Spanish Colonial Churches of Yucatan*. Santa Barbara, CA: Espadaña Press, 1988.

Plunket, Patricia, and Gabriela Uruñuela. "Appeasing the Volcano Gods." *Archaeology*, July/August 1998: 36–42.

Recinos, Adrián and Delia Goetz. *The Annals of The Cakchiquels*. Norman, OK: University of Oklahoma Press, 1953.

Recinos, Adrián. *The Book of the People: Popol Vuh*. Translated by Delia Goetz and Sylvanus Morley. Los Angeles: The Plantin Press, 1954.

Redfield, Robert M., trans. *The Folk Culture of Yucatan*. Chicago: The University of Chicago Press, 1941.

Reina, Ruben E. *Shadows: A Mayan Way of Knowing*. New York: New Horizon Press, 1984.

Restall, Matthew. *Maya Conquistador*. Boston: Beacon Press, 1998.

Rosa, Rodrigo Rey. *Dust on Her Tongue*. Translated by Paul Bowles. San Francisco: City Light Books, 1992.

Sabloff, Jeremy A. *The New Archaeology and the Ancient Maya*. New York: Scientific American Library, 1990.

Schele, Linda and David Freidel. *A Forest of Kings: The Untold Story of the Ancient Maya*. New York: William Morrow and Company, 1990.

Schele, Linda and Mary Ellen Miller. *The Blood of Kings: Dynasty and Ritual in Maya Art*. New York: George Braziller, Inc., and Kimbell Art Museum, 1986.

Schuster, Angela M.H. "Rituals of the Modern Maya." *Archaeology*. July/August 1997: 50-53.

Sexton, James D. *Campesino: The Diary of a Guatemalan Indian*. Tucson, AZ: The University of Arizona Press, 1985.

Sharer, Robert J. *The Ancient Maya*. 5th ed. Stanford, CA: Stanford University Press, 1994.

Smith, Carol A., ed. *Guatemalan Indians and The State: 1540 to 1988*. Austin: University of Texas Press, 1994.

Stephens, John L. *Incidents of Travel in Central America, Chiapas and Yucatan*. New York: Dover Publications, 1969.

Stuart, George E. "The Royal Crypts of Copán." *National Geographic*. December 1997: 68-93.

Suhler, Charles, and David Freidel. "Life and Death in A Maya War Zone." *Archaeology*. May/June 1998: 28-34.

Sullivan, Paul. *Unfinished Conversations: Mayas and Foreigners between Two Wars*. Berkeley: University of California Press, 1989.

Tate, Carolyn E. *Yaxchilan: The Design of a Maya Ceremonial City*. Austin: University of Texas Press, 1992.

Tedlock, Barbara. *Time and the Highland Maya*. Albuquerque: University of New Mexico Press, 1982.

Tedlock, Dennis. *Popol Vuh: The Mayan Book of the Dawn of Life*. New York: Simon and Schuster, 1986.

Thompson, J. Eric S. *Maya History and Religion*. Norman, OK: University of Oklahoma Press, 1970.

Villatoro, Marcos McPeek. *Walking to La Milpa: Living in Guatemala with Armies, Demons, Abrazos, and Death*. Kingston, RI: Moyer Bell, 1996.

Vogt, Evon Z. *Tortillas for the Gods*. Norman, OK: University of Oklahoma Press, 1993.